Igor Stravinsky

A Brief Guide to His Life and Work

DAVID EWEN

Text originally published in David Ewen's
"Twentieth Century Composers"
Copyright © 1937 Thomas Y. Crowell Company

ISBN: 978-1544915364

A. J. Cornell Publications

On May 29, 1913, a volcanic eruption rocked musical Paris.

The eruption was caused by the first performance of the *Sacre du Printemps (The Rite of Spring)* at the Théâtre des Champs Élysées, an offering of the Diaghilev Ballet Russe, headed by Nijinsky. However, it was not Diaghilev's original choreographic conception that caused the tremors among the audience, or even the exotic theme of the ballet itself, heightened by the bizarre settings and costume designs of Nicholas Roerich. Rather, it was the musical score, drenched with strange colors and defiantly new sounds, a score sublimely indifferent to tradition and heritage, fearlessly pronouncing a fresh vocabulary and what then appeared to be a strangely distorted one. The music was the work of the young Igor Stravinsky, who had already made his mark with two other ballets also presented by the Diaghilev troupe.

The music had not progressed beyond several minutes, under Pierre Monteux's baton, when a growling began to be heard in the audience. The music seemed to lack altogether the logic and coherence that is ordinarily expected of a creative work. There was no recognizable melody, only distorted lines of sound that zigzagged aimlessly, so it seemed, through a score complicated by a labyrinth of rhythm and sporadic outbursts of cacophony. As the sounds became more confused, restless movement was heard in the seats, some snickers from the audience, some smothered guffaws. Before long, the air of the theatre became charged with electric excitation, and the sparks of dissension ignited the passion of the listeners. "A certain part of the audience," writes Carl van Vechten, who was a member of that historic assemblage, "was thrilled by what it considered to be a blasphemous attempt to destroy music as an art and, swept away with wrath, began, very soon after the rise of the curtain, to make cat-calls and to offer audible suggestions as to how the performance should proceed. The orchestra played unheard except occasionally, when a slight lull occurred. The young man seated behind me in a box stood up during the course of the ballet to enable him to see more clearly. The intense excitement under which he was laboring betrayed itself when he began to beat rhythmically on the top of my head with fists. My emotion was so great that I did not feel the blows for some time."

While the music was in progress, a lady stretched into the box neighboring hers and slapped the face of a man who was hissing; her escort arose, cards were exchanged, and a duel took place the following morning. Saint-Saëns viciously denounced the composer;

André Capu, the critic, bellowed that it was all a colossal bluff, while at the same time Maurice Ravel was crying "genius" at his inattentive neighbors. The Austrian Ambassador laughed loudly in derision; Florent Schmitt, the composer, attacked him for his laughter. The Princesse de Pourtalès left her box exclaiming: "I am sixty years old, but this is the first time that anyone has dared to make a fool of me!" Another proud society lady rose majestically in her seat, contracted her capacious bosom and spat in the face of one of the demonstrators. In the wings, Stravinsky was clinging to Nijinsky's collar in an attempt to prevent the dancer from rushing upon the stage and expressing openly his contempt of the audience. And throughout it all, Claude Debussy, pale and trembling, was pleading to the audience to remain quiet and listen patiently to the music.

At the time of the *Sacre* "scandal," Igor Stravinsky was thirty-one years old, a brusque, ungainly young man, slight of build, whose somewhat awkward and self-conscious mannerisms had not as yet been polished by Parisian refinement. His upper lip was still clean-shaven, his face, in consequence, seeming longer and leaner than it has in more recent years. A *pince-nez*, perched at a sharp angle on the bridge of his nose, gave him a professorial appearance.

His reputation had been imposing even before the riot of the *Sacre* brought him worldwide notoriety. His name had already been linked with the rising futurist movement: in Rome, the redoubtable Marinetti had carried a banner in the streets proclaiming: "Down with Wagner; long live Stravinsky!" To a meager handful of younger art-lovers, chafing under the bondage of formalism and tradition, the name of Stravinsky had already become a shibboleth. The *Sacre,* therefore, had established more firmly what *Petrushka* had first created two years before this— namely, Stravinsky's reputation as the enfant terrible in the music of his time.

The *Sacre du Printemps,* with its attendant riot, brought to a climax an artistic career that had been meteoric. Igor Stravinsky was born in Oranienbaum, a suburb of St. Petersburg, on St. Igor's Day, June 5, 1882. At the time of Stravinsky's birth, Glinka, the father of Russian music, had been dead twenty-five years; his influence, however, had already produced the school of national music known as the "Russian Five." By 1882, the "Russian Five" were at the height of their creative growth (except Moussorgsky, who had died the year before). They had already formed, molded, and developed a musical speech that Stravinsky was soon to inherit. Borodin was forty-eight; behind him was the composition of the Symphony in B minor, the String Quartet in A and the remarkable tone-poem, *In the Steppes of Central Asia.* Balakireff, aged forty-six, had already produced his *Tamara* and *Russ.* Moussorgsky's *Boris Godounoff* produced successfully eight years before, was still some two decades from acceptance as a Russian epic. Nikolai Rimsky-Korsakoff was the only one of the "Five" whose future still stretched before him; and Rimsky-Korsakoff, then in his thirty-ninth year, had already created the

Antar symphony and *Sniegouroutchka*. Stravinsky, therefore, was born at a time when musical activity was richly productive in Russia.

Igor Stravinsky's father, Feodor, was a well-known singer of the Maryinsky Theatre, who—as though to establish a more direct link between Igor and the traditions of the "Russian Five"—had been cast as the drunken monk in the first performance of *Boris Godounoff*. Feodor Stravinsky, despite his artistic calling, was a practical, levelheaded man. Long before Igor's birth he had decided that any child of his would be strongly discouraged from adopting art as a profession; for Igor, therefore, he had selected law. Feodor Stravinsky, moreover, possessed a strong streak of stubbornness together with his level head. In his early academic studies, Igor was very nearly hopeless (the schoolmaster at one time dispatched a note to Feodor Stravinsky prophesying that Igor would never amount to anything!) while in his piano study he revealed an alert intelligence; but not even these facts could persuade the father to change the plans he had conceived. Clinging to them tenaciously, he saw Igor through preparatory school and finally into the University of St. Petersburg.

From his earliest years, Stravinsky showed unusual responsiveness to music. He received his first vivid musical impressions as a mere child, from performances of Glinka's *A Life for the Tsar* and *Russlan and Ludmilla*, and of Tchaikovsky's *Symphonie Pathétique;* these impressions were so vivid that Stravinsky never forgot them. He was a frequent visitor at the home of his uncle, where performances of German works took place regularly. He likewise attended public concerts—particularly those of the Imperial Music Society, directed by Nápravnik, and of the Russian Symphony Orchestra (which, in 1885, had been founded by Belaiev).

His music study, however, was spasmodic. As a child of nine he began to have piano lessons. Then, hearing one day a piano recital of Josef Hofmann, he was inspired to study the instrument with greater assiduity and industry. In a few years, he succeeded in attaining a supple technique.

During his University days, he received the permission of his father to begin the study of harmony under a private tutor. Dull exercises and implacable rules were of small attraction to him; in a short while, he discontinued the study. In his eighteenth year, he began to thumb a text on counterpoint, finding therein so much fascination that he assumed the study of the subject by himself. He achieved a remarkable knowledge of its technique, particularly in view of the fact that he studied it without the help of a teacher.

When Stravinsky was twenty years old, he left with his family for Bad Wildungen, Germany, for a prolonged holiday. While there, he heard that Rimsky-Korsakoff was in Heidelberg. A great admirer of the composer and teacher, Stravinsky left immediately for Heidelberg to consult Rimsky-Korsakoff about his own career. He performed for the master a few abortive piano pieces which he had recently composed. To Rimsky-Korsakoff, these pieces represented the self-conscious stammerings of an immature musical mind; however, behind them Rimsky-Korsakoff perceived an original message and the rudiments of an individual speech. He therefore urged Stravinsky to continue his musical activity, dissuaded him from entering the St. Petersburg Conservatory, whose rigid curriculum, he feared, might be unbearable to so headstrong a personality, and advised the young composer to submit to him whatever he produced.

Rimsky-Korsakoff's praise—couched though it was in a cautious and none too enthusiastic vocabulary—convinced Stravinsky, at last, that he could become a serious musician. He did not, as yet, abandon law. Instead, in his spare hours, he hurled himself with youthful zest into the artistic life of St. Petersburg. He read avidly the art-journal, *The World of Art*, edited by an apostle of modernism, Diaghilev. Frequently, he visited the exhibition of paintings that this very same Diaghilev arranged in St. Petersburg. And he became an enthusiastic member of a progressive musical society that regularly performed the chamberworks of such modern French composers as Debussy, César Franck, Paul Dukas, Chabrier and Gabriel Fauré.

Towards the close of 1903, Stravinsky had completed his first unified composition, a piano sonata. For a fortnight, he lived with Rimsky-Korsakoff, while the master carefully and patiently dissected the work and mercilessly disclosed its technical weaknesses. Rimsky-Korsakoff found that the composition, though the work of an undeveloped musician, possessed a strength of fiber and an intensity of speech not frequently discovered in a first-born work. He therefore no longer had any hesitancy in advising Stravinsky to take the final step—exchange the profession of law for that of music.

In 1906 Stravinsky was married to his cousin, a girl of unusual intelligence who was strongly instrumental in swaying him from a legal career to that of music. Early in 1905, upon completing his course at the University, he had definitely changed the direction of his life. Brushing aside the legal profession permanently, he began a two-year period of intensive study of instrumentation under Rimsky-Korsakoff. And under the guidance of the master, he was converted from a raw student into a self-confident musician.

The first fruits of his studies with Rimsky-Korsakoff were the Symphony in E-flat, dedicated to his teacher, and a suite for voice and orchestra after three poems of Pushkin, entitled *Faune et Bergère*, both composed between 1906 and 1907. In these works, the future rebel had not yet begun to flaunt his defiance in the face of tradition. This was music strongly influenced by the idiom established by the "Russian Five," couched in orthodox forms. One critic found the Symphony a "straightforward work which is chiefly notable for its docile acquiescence in conventionality to a degree that almost contradicts the report of his chafing under academic restraint." The Symphony and the *Faune et Bergère* were first performed privately by the court orchestra in 1907. Shortly after this, the Belaiev concerts of the Russian Symphony

Orchestra had the distinction of giving the first public performance of a work by Stravinsky when it introduced *Faune et Bergère*.

Stravinsky next set to work upon a *Scherzo fantastique*, for orchestra—inspired by Maurice Maeterlinck's *Life of the Bee*—and upon the first act of an opera, *Le Rossignol*, based on the famous fairy-tale of Andersen. Rimsky-Korsakoff saw the sketches of both compositions, approved of them highly, and for the first time enthusiastically prophesied a brilliant career for the young composer. In 1908, Stravinsky abandoned the composition of his opera to write the *Feu d'artifice (Fireworks)*, music prepared in honor of the forthcoming marriage of Rimsky-Korsakoff's daughter, Sonia. He dispatched the manuscript to the master as a surprise offering for the wedding. The master, however, never saw the work. The package was returned to Stravinsky unopened, "on account of the death of the addressee."

The death of Rimsky-Korsakoff was a hard blow to Stravinsky, who had lost a great teacher and a great friend. In expression of his profound sentiments, and as a gesture of farewell, Stravinsky composed a *Chant funèbre*.

The winter of 1908 was a turning point in the career of Igor Stravinsky. At that time the Siloti concerts in St. Petersburg presented the *Scherzo fantastique* and the *Feu d'artifice*. In the audience was Diaghilev, increasingly famous sponsor of modern art and organizer of a new Russian ballet that was to be introduced to Paris the following year. Diaghilev, who possessed an uncanny sensitiveness to the presence of hitherto undetected genius, recognized that greatness lurked in the hidden corners of these works. Immature they were, to be sure; but Diaghilev had too penetrating a vision not to perceive behind their immaturity the growing stature of a striking individuality, particularly in the brilliantly orchestrated *Feu d'artifice*, of which Fokine, the ballet-master, once said that it always made him see vividly flames searing the skies. Diaghilev, therefore, approached Stravinsky after the concert, asked him if he would be interested in enlisting his talent in the Diaghilev ballet, and—as a first assignment— commissioned Stravinsky to orchestrate two Chopin pieces to be used in the ballet, *Chopiniana* (later renamed *Les Sylphides*). Thus began a relationship which, continuing for two decades, was to have an enormous effect not only upon Stravinsky's artistic evolution but upon the development of modern music as well.

At the time of this first meeting with Stravinsky, Diaghilev was thirty-six years old, his reputation— after many tribulations—solidly established at last both in Russia and in Paris. In his youth he had revealed an alert and supple intelligence keenly sensitive to beauty in whatever form or medium it was expressed. He turned first to music, aspiring to become a composer, but—after a heartbreaking interview with Rimsky-Korsakoff—was convinced that musical creation was not his forte. From music he turned to art and journalism. He founded and edited a progressive magazine, *The World of Art*, which publicized European art-movements among the Russian intelligentsia; and he inaugurated annual art exhibitions in which he introduced Russian art lovers for the first time to some of the most characteristic products of the various schools of modern European art.

Finally, after an extended period in which his principal goal was the education of Russia in European art trends (a period whose importance to Russia's artistic development should not be underestimated), Diaghilev suddenly was imbued with a far more intoxicating mission. He had recently rediscovered Russian art, and found therein artistic values and concepts that he felt were unique and incomparable. He, therefore, appointed himself as the prophet to introduce and interpret this art to the rest of Europe.

In 1906 Diaghilev held an imposing exhibition of modern Russian painting in Paris. The tremendous success of this venture gave Diaghilev the strength to expand his program and redouble his activity. In 1907 he arranged a series of historical concerts of Russian music in Paris, consisting of the foremost examples of Russian symphonic and operatic art. Glazunov, Rachmaninoff and Rimsky-Korsakoff personally conducted programs of their own works. Josef Hofmann played the piano concertos of Scriabin and Liapounov, while Rachmaninoff performed his own Second Concerto. Scenes from Borodin's *Prince Igor* and Moussorgsky's *Boris Godounoff* were featured, with Feodor Chaliapin making his first appearances in Paris.

But Diaghilev had only begun. In 1908 he brought

to Paris the complete Moussorgsky opera, *Boris Godounoff*, with Feodor Chaliapin in the principal role—the scenery, costumes and choreography personally supervised by Diaghilev. This was the first indication Diaghilev had given of his instinctive knowledge of the theatre and of his genius for organization. *Boris Godounoff* was a decided success.

From opera to ballet was but a short step for Diaghilev. A casual conversation at a café, in which Diaghilev boasted of the unique distinction of Russian dancing, inspired him to bring its finest examples to Paris. In 1909, therefore, the Diaghilev Ballet Russe came into being in Paris. Fokine was ballet-master; the principal dancers included Karsavina, Anna Pavlova and Nijinsky. And from the very first the guiding genius was Diaghilev.

Diaghilev was no mere dabbler in the arts. In his own way he was as much a creator as those eminent collaborators whom he gathered under his wing for the Ballet Russe. A dilettante in the finest meaning of the word, he was, as his biographer wrote of him, "a master painter who never painted, a master musician who never wrote or played, a master dancer who never danced or devised the steps of a ballet." An artistic instinct that seemed infallible, an impeccable taste, an insight of penetrating sharpness—these things combined to make him that organizing genius that could blend the innumerable parts of a ballet into a completely unified artistic whole. And like all true geniuses, Diaghilev had the power to electrify and inspire all those with whom he came into contact:

members of his ballet frequently confessed that when Diaghilev was not witnessing a performance, the quality of the dancing deteriorated noticeably.

It was this dynamic and revitalizing personality, this cultured and eclectic mind, broad enough to encompass all of the arts, who crossed Stravinsky's path in 1908.

How important an influence Diaghilev was in Stravinsky's evolution has been the subject for many copious paragraphs. Certainly it is ridiculous to assume that had there been no Diaghilev there would have been no Stravinsky—an assertion that many of Diaghilev's devotees have strongly and frequently reiterated. There are sufficient foreshadowings of the later Stravinsky in the *Scherzo fantastique* and *Feu d'artifice*—particularly in the nervous energy of the rhythms, the electrically charged instrumentation, and above all in the first signs of impatience and dissatisfaction with existing musical conventions—to convince us that Stravinsky would have made his mark without Diaghilev. However, it would be just as naïve to disregard Diaghilev's influence entirely. An immature genius does not almost overnight evolve into an integrated artist with a fully developed, highly personal vocabulary, without the influence of a powerful external stimulus. The only convincing explanation of why Stravinsky reached full maturity so rapidly, why two such works as *Feu d'artifice* and *L'Oiseau de feu (The Fire-Bird)* were separated by only two years, is— Diaghilev.

Chopiniana—with the two Stravinsky orchestrations

commissioned by Diaghilev—was featured in the inaugural season of the Ballet Russe at the Paris Opéra. The orchestration pleased Diaghilev considerably—so much so that, several months later, in planning another season for his Ballet Russe, he decided to yield to one of his characteristic extravagant gestures by placing his most important musical commission in the hands of this young and inexperienced composer—even though the foremost of Russian composers were eager to serve him.

Diaghilev had been revolving in his mind a plan to translate the famous legend of the Fire-Bird into a ballet. It is for this ballet that Stravinsky was commissioned to compose an original score.

During late winter of 1909 and early spring of 1910, Stravinsky worked industriously upon his first major assignment—the ballet-master Fokine, who fashioned the scenario of the *Fire-Bird*, almost indefatigably at his side. "They worked very closely together, phrase by phrase. Stravinsky brought him a beautiful cantilena on the entrance of the Tsarevitch into the garden of the girls with the golden apples. But Fokine disapproved. 'No, no!' he said. 'You bring him in like a tenor. Break the phrase where he merely shows his head on his first intrusion. Then make the curious swish of the garden's magic horse's return, and then, when he shows his hand again, bring in the full swing of the melody.' " (Lincoln Kirstein in his biography, *Fokine*.)

Stravinsky's score was finally completed in May of 1910. One month later, on June 25th, it was given its première at the Paris Opéra by the Ballet Russe. The principal dancers included Fokine, Mme. Fokina, and Karsavina; the settings were designed by Bakst and Golovine; and the conductor was Gabriel Pierné.

The scenario of Fokine follows closely the traditional Russian legend, and serves admirably as the program for the concert suite, *L'Oiseau de feu,* which is usually performed in the symphony hall. Ivan Tsarevitch, roaming aimlessly one night, stumbles across the Fire-Bird and captures it as it is in the act of plucking golden fruit from a silver tree. As a reward for its release, the Fire-Bird presents Ivan with one of its glowing feathers, which he accepts. Suddenly, the thick darkness of the night dissipates. A castle comes clearly into view, from whose portals emerge thirteen maidens of surpassing beauty. Little realizing that they are being observed, they play with the silver tree and its golden fruit. Emerging from hiding, Ivan receives from one of the maidens a golden fruit as gift, and they dance out of sight. The night passes into dawn. Suddenly, Ivan realizes that the castle is the home of the dreaded Kastcheï, who captures wayfaring travelers and subjects them to his spell. Determined to conquer this monster, Ivan enters the castle, which is guarded by terrifying monsters. Kastcheï attempts to bewitch Ivan; but his power is impotent before the magic feather that Ivan holds in his hand. Then the Fire-Bird comes to view, reveals to Ivan a casket and informs him that Kastcheï's fate is concealed therein. Ivan opens the casket, and withdraws an egg, which he smashes to the ground. Death emerges from the smashed eggshell and obsesses the body of Kastcheï. As Kastcheï perishes, the castle suddenly disappears, and the maidens are freed from their bondage. As a reward, Ivan receives in marriage the hand of the most beautiful of the captive maidens.

L'Oiseau de feu was an instantaneous success, the most substantial triumph of the 1910 season of the Ballet Russe. Diaghilev was thrilled by Stravinsky's score, and knew instantly that he had made no mistake in recruiting the young composer as his principal music collaborator. Some of the critics were puzzled by several of the more unorthodox pages of Stravinsky's music, but for the most part they found it full of power and beauty. A handful of French musicians knew that with the *L'Oiseau* a formidable musical creator had emerged. One of these was Claude Debussy who, immediately after the first performance, rushed backstage, embraced Stravinsky, and poured out his effusive congratulations before the embarrassed young composer

L'Oiseau de feu was Stravinsky's first significant thrust towards individuality and greatness. His first creative period—the period of apprenticeship that produced the Symphony, the *Scherzo fantastique* and *Feu d'artifice*—was now definitely over. He was at last well started in formulating his own idiom; he had begun to show those personal mannerisms that were to become the revealing fingerprints on all the works of his second period.

In these works of the middle phase of Stravinsky's artistic development—ranging from *L'Oiseau* to *Les*

Noces (The Wedding)—Stravinsky is essentially the Russian, his musical speech heavy with a Russian accent. His second period stemmed from the soil of the "Russian Five," from Moussorgsky and Rimsky-Korsakoff particularly; *L'Oiseau de feu,* as a matter of fact, is a recognizable godson of Rimsky-Korsakoff's influence. Russian folk-music obsesses Stravinsky in the works of this time. While he borrows directly from folk-music only rarely, his melodic and harmonic material have an unmistakable Russian character. They are full of the spirit and color of Russian folk-song.

In comparison with *Le Sacre du Printemps* and *Les Noces, L'Oiseau de feu* may appear conservative, indeed. But, in 1910, it stung and pinched musical ears, unaccustomed to such brazen audacities. True, Stravinsky permitted himself the luxury of tender, delicate, often poignantly beautiful melody—as in the *Dance of the Princesses* and the *Berceuse*—which belongs more to the equipment of the "Russian Five" than to that of a rebel composer. Yet, at other moments, an already striking impatience with old norms asserts itself. In the *Dance of the King Kastcheï* there is already a rhythmic barbarism that, in its nervous energy and agitation, sweeps convention to the winds. The brusque leaps and starts of Stravinsky's later melodic line frequently pierce through the prevailingly smoother texture of *L'Oiseau.* And it has that characteristic Stravinsky orchestration, as luminous as flame.

The success of *L'Oiseau de feu* definitely established the Ballet Russe as an annual feature of the Paris theatrical season. In planning the 1911 season, therefore, Diaghilev inevitably looked upon Stravinsky to furnish him with a new score. There had already been some conversation between Stravinsky and Diaghilev about a ballet theme that was later to reach realization in *Le Sacre du Printemps*. Stravinsky, however, was mentally and physically too exhausted by the strain of composing *L'Oiseau* to undertake another arduous assignment. Instead, he sought relaxation by composing a work in a lighter vein, a sort of *Konzertstück* for piano and orchestra.

The one great obstacle facing Stravinsky, in the sketching of this work, was the selection of an appropriate programmatic title. *"Konzertstück"* was, after all, too effete a name for a work of such malicious irony as Stravinsky was etching; and Stravinsky felt that, unless he succeeded in finding a suitably descriptive designation for his work, its progress would be greatly retarded. For hours at a stretch he walked along the edge of the Lake of Geneva, whistling to himself snatches of his new music as he exhausted his imagination and experience for a title. When it finally came to him, it literally burst upon his consciousness when he least expected it. But it was precisely the theme for which, instinctively, he had been groping. He would call his new work *Petrushka* after the pathetic sawdust puppet, well known to the Russian fair.

The progress of *Petrushka* was temporarily interrupted in the spring of 1911 when Stravinsky suffered a severe illness, the result of nicotine poisoning. For a period, it was seriously thought that he was on the border of death. But in the end recovery brought him an altogether new zest for composition, and returning to the manuscript of *Petrushka* he felt the pen fly under his fingertips.

In the summer of 1911, Diaghilev visited Stravinsky at his home in Clarens, Switzerland, for the purpose of hearing portions of *Le Sacre,* which he believed Stravinsky to be composing at the time. At first very much surprised to hear that not *Le Sacre* but a substitute was awaiting him, Diaghilev nevertheless listened patiently to Stravinsky's exposition of the *Petrushka* subject, and to those portions which Stravinsky had already committed to paper. *Petrushka* instantly exhilarated and excited Diaghilev. He recognized in the subject a ballet cut to the pattern of the Ballet Russe requirements; as he listened to sections of the music he envisioned in his mind's eye Nijinsky as Petrushka, capering to the pungent rhythmic patterns and the wittily satirical phrases of Stravinsky's music.

Stravinsky completed *Petrushka: Scènes burlesques en 4 tableaux* in Rome in May, 1911. On June 13 the Ballet Russe introduced it at the Châtelet, in Paris. Karsavina and Nijinsky were the principal dancers; the scenery was painted by Benois; Fokine was the balletmaster, and Pierre Monteux the conductor.

The scenario of Petrushka had been prepared by Alexandre Benois. "This ballet depicts the life of the lower classes in Russia with all its dissoluteness, barbarity, tragedy and misery. Petrushka is a sort of Polichinello, a poor hero always suffering from the cruelty of the police and every kind of wrong and unjust persecution. This represents symbolically the whole tragedy in the existence of the Russian people, a suffering from despotism and injustice. The scene is laid in the midst of the Russian carnival, and the streets are lined with booths, in one of which Petrushka plays a kind of humorous role. He is killed, but he appears again as a ghost on the roof of the booth to frighten his enemy, his old employer, an allusion to the despotic rule in Russia." (This excerpt is quoted by Philip Hale in his admirable program notes on *Petrushka*. The source of this quotation, however, is not given.)

Petrushka definitely established Stravinsky's fame. Once again, his unusual effects—now grown more startlingly original and bizarre—caused the raising of eyebrows. But many music critics could not deny Stravinsky's seductively fresh approach, the rich Slavic flavor of his musical material and, most important of all, his ability to give music an expressiveness that few, if any, of his contemporaries could equal. To the public at large, Stravinsky represented much more an intriguing but ephemeral novelty than a permanent influence; his music appeared more original than important. But a handful of musicians and art-lovers already accepted him as a prophet of the future.

Following *Petrushka*, Stravinsky began work upon *Le Sacre du Printemps*. Plans for *Le Sacre* had been conceived two years earlier, as Stravinsky himself informs us. "One day, when I was finishing the last pages of *L'Oiseau de feu* in St. Petersburg, I had a fleeting vision which came to me as a complete surprise, my mind at the moment being full of other things. I saw in imagination a solemn pagan rite: sage elders, seated in a circle, watched a young girl dance herself to death. They were sacrificing her to propitiate the god of spring. Such was the theme of the *Sacre du Printemps*. I must confess that this vision made a deep impression upon me and I at once described it to my friend, Nicholas Roerich, he being a painter who had specialized in pagan subjects. He welcomed my inspiration with enthusiasm, and became my collaborator in this creation. In Paris, I told Diaghilev about it, and he was at once carried away by the idea, though its realization was delayed. . . ." *(Stravinsky: An Autobiography.)*

The completion of *Le Sacre* was momentarily interrupted in the summer of 1912 when Stravinsky left with Diaghilev for Bayreuth to witness a performance of Wagner's *Parsifal*. *Parsifal* sickened Stravinsky both as a theatrical spectacle and as a musical score. His utter distaste for Wagner's music has remained something of an obsession with him throughout his career.

Le Sacre du Printemps, performed at the Théâtre des Champs Elysées on May 29, 1913, definitely established Stravinsky as a world figure in music—a man who from that day became one of the most publicized and controversial personalities of our generation. However, though *Le Sacre* had been subject for derision and laughter, Stravinsky was convinced that he had produced an important work; he insisted that he was right and his critics wrong. And, slowly and inevitably, Stravinsky's faith in himself and in his work was to receive eloquent justification. On July 11,

1913, Pierre Monteux introduced the ballet to London; while there was some hissing, there was infinitely more applause. On April 5, 1914, Pierre Monteux conducted the music of the ballet at a symphonic concert at the Casino de Paris; the enthusiasm was stirring. Since that time, *Le Sacre du Printemps* has been accepted by the world of music as the crowning work of Stravinsky's career, and one of the indisputable monuments of twentieth century music.

Two more important works, with roots deeply embedded in Russian tradition, succeeded *Le Sacre*. In 1914 Stravinsky completed his opera *Le Chant du rossignol (The Song of the Nightingale)*, the first act of which he had planned and sketched in Russia in 1909. S. Mitoussov fashioned the libretto after the Andersen fairy-tale. The opera was performed for the first time at the Paris Opéra in May of 1914, with only moderate success. During the War, Stravinsky converted the opera into a ballet, omitting much material from the first act. This ballet—with scenery by Matisse and choreography by Massine—was presented by the Ballet Russe in Paris on February 2, 1920. The orchestral suite drawn from the ballet has become familiar on orchestra programs.

Stravinsky's orchestral suite follows the narrative of the fairy-tale closely. The Emperor of China, hearing tales of the beautiful singing of a brown nightingale, invites it to his court. The bird sings so beautifully that the hearts of all the courtiers are softened and the eyes of the Emperor are filled with tears. But suddenly an envoy arrives bearing a mechanical nightingale that delights the entire court with its ingenious albeit stilted song. Heartbroken, the brown bird flies out of the palace and disappears. Enraged, the Emperor permanently banishes the nightingale from his empire. Shortly after this, the Emperor is at the threshold of death, and the physicians have given up all hope. One morning, the brown nightingale flies through the window and sings at the Emperor's bed so beautifully that she softens the heart of Death, who leaves the royal bedside. The courtiers return, expecting to find their Emperor dead, only to see him glowing with health and contentment.

The last of Stravinsky's important Russian works, bringing the second period to termination, was *Les Noces,* "scènes chorégraphiques Russes." *Les Noces* was composed during one of the most trying periods of Stravinsky's life. He began the first sketches in London in 1914, when the War suddenly forced him to flee with his family to Switzerland. There followed several years of great financial distress, heightened when the Russian revolutionists confiscated his last possessions. Troubles never coming single-handed, Stravinsky was also suffering excruciating pain as a result of intercostal neuralgia, which made breathing difficult and which even brought on partial paralysis of the legs. At the same time, his spirits were depressed by the death of a younger brother and a nurse whom he had accepted as a foster-mother. In the midst of such confusion and bitterness—further heightened not a little by the inconvenience of being forced to compose a great part of his work in a cold

Swiss attic, cluttered with empty Suchard chocolate boxes—Stravinsky created his tonal picture of a peasant wedding in Russia.

Les Noces, which was completed in 1917, did not receive its final instrumentation until 1923. On June 13, 1923, the Ballet Russe introduced it at the Paris Opéra to thunderous acclaim. It was esteemed as one of the greatest artistic triumphs of the Ballet Russe and one of Stravinsky's most vitally dynamic scores.

Stravinsky's middle creative period had spanned seven years, in which five major works were produced. It is the opinion of more than one authority that it is in this period that Stravinsky fashioned his greatest music, music in which the abortive revolutions of the "Russian Five" were brought to their ultimate and inevitable destination. In these five works, harmonic language had been immeasurably enriched, contrapuntal writing had been stretched to its utmost flexibility, forms had become elastically supple, orchestration had been illuminated with electric brilliance, rhythm had been treated with a new and dynamic freshness. In these works, Stravinsky created an impression of irresistible energy. This music gives the listener the impression that it was created at white heat. The music sweeps relentlessly along like a typhoon. Stravinsky's works from *L'Oiseau de feu* through *Les Noces* are the irrepressible outbursts of creative genius.

In 1919 Stravinsky took up his residence in Garches, in the environs of Paris, and from this time on his permanent home was France. At the same time,

Stravinsky applied for French citizenship.

But in his music, he had already changed his nationality. Beginning with *Renard*—a "burlesque from Russian folk-tales" for four male voices and chamber orchestra, composed in 1917—a mystifying metamorphosis came over Stravinsky's style and idiom. Stravinsky had suddenly discarded the style of his magnificent second period as though it were a removable cloak, and assumed an altogether new and foreign one. Russian tradition and culture no longer dominated his thinking; from the composition of music that clearly showed its Slavic origins he turned to the creation of works whose polished surfaces reflected the elegance of French art. Most important of all, he had ceased being the defiant rebel, the fearless pioneer. Renouncing his former vitriolic style, he began to compose music with a simplified and lucid texture, in forms polished and refined. A cool counterpoint replaced his former tangled rhythms; his orchestration had now been peeled of several layers of color; the former nervous excitation now yielded to an aloof placidity. Stravinsky was composing "in the style of Handel and Scarlatti."

Renard launched Stravinsky upon his third period as a creator, a period even more radically different from the one that preceded it than the second had been from the first. With two burlesques—*L'Histoire du soldat,* for chamber orchestra, "a story to be read, played and danced" (introduced at Lausanne on September 28, 1918) and *Pulcinella,* a ballet based upon melodic material of Pergolesi (first performed by the

Ballet Russe at the Paris Opéra on May 15, 1920)—and with the Concerto for Piano and Orchestra, composed in 1923–24 and introduced in the latter year in Paris by Serge Koussevitzky with the composer at the piano, the new style reached crystallization. Stravinsky's music was now completely objective, unemotional, restrained; it was, in short, "pure" music. "I loathe orchestral effects as means of embellishment," Stravinsky said, a few years later, in an interview. "I have long since renounced the futilities of *brio*. I dislike cajoling the public; it inconveniences me. . . . The crowd expects the artist to tear out his entrails and exhibit them. That is what is held to be the noblest expression of art, and called personality, individuality, temperament, and so on." Certainly, Stravinsky had no further intention of indulging in emotional exhibitionism; the music of his new period was as impersonal as a slab of marble.

In 1925 Stravinsky crossed the ocean for the first time. The leading orchestras of America—including the New York Philharmonic Orchestra—were placed in his hands; in a series of guest concerts, Stravinsky conducted programs devoted to his own music. The regal reception which America gave him showed clearly that, although Stravinsky had changed his aesthetic philosophy and reversed his style completely, he was still, in the eyes of the music public of America, the most picturesque and glamorous figure among the composers of our time.

In 1927 Stravinsky composed his first major work in the new idiom, an opera-oratorio based upon

Sophocles' *Oedipus Rex*. In planning the work, Stravinsky felt strongly that the text, to suit best the quality of his music, must be in a classical tongue. Ancient Greek he discarded as a language that was too dead. He therefore selected Latin. Thus the text, which was written by Jean Cocteau, was translated into Latin by Jean Daniélou. In this form it was first performed by the Ballet Russe in Paris at the Théâtre Sarah Bernhardt on May 30, 1927.

One year later, upon a commission from Mrs. Elizabeth Sprague Coolidge, the eminent American patron of music, Stravinsky composed another classical work—this time for chamber orchestra, *Apollon Musagète*. *Apollon* was the first work of Stravinsky to be given its world premiere in America (it was performed at the concerts of the Library of Congress in Washington, D.C., in May of 1928). It was also the last work of Stravinsky featured by the Ballet Russe. In 1929, Diaghilev died in Venice. And with Diaghilev gone, Stravinsky's last link with the Ballet Russe was permanently severed.

After *Apollon* came two more outstanding works. In 1930, Stravinsky composed the *Symphonie des Psaumes (The Symphony of Psalms)*, for chorus and orchestra, inscribed to "the great glory of God" and dedicated to the Boston Symphony Orchestra, which had commissioned the work to celebrate the organization's fiftieth anniversary. The *Symphonie*, however, was not given its first performance by the Boston Symphony Orchestra. Through a mishandling of the dates, it was first performed by the Brussels Philharmonic Society on December 13, 1930, six days before Koussevitzky introduced it in Boston. The text of the *Symphonie* is from the Vulgate. In 1933–34 Stravinsky produced a "melodrama," *Perséphone*, for chorus, orchestra, tenor and speaking voice, composed to a text of André Gide. Commissioned by Ida Rubinstein, it was introduced by her in Paris in April, 1934.

More recently, Stravinsky has composed a choreographic drama—*Jeu de cartes en trois donnes (The Card Party)*—dealing with the game of poker. Composed expressly for the American Ballet, this work was first introduced by that organization at the Metropolitan Opera House, on April 27, 1937. The action of the ballet portrays a game of cards by several choreographic and pantomimic devices. The stage is set like a great club-room, but the action, representing the card game, takes place on an elevated, smaller stage. The face cards and the joker are represented by solo dancers, costumed to the subject. This was the first time when a Stravinsky ballet had had its world premiere in America. It was conducted by the composer. Two earlier ballets shared the program—*Apollon Musagète* and *La Baiser de la Fée.*

There has been as much acrimonious disagreement about the importance of Stravinsky's neo-classical idiom as there was, in 1913, about the artistic importance of *Le Sacre.* Today, as well as in 1913, Stravinsky is a subject for debate. On the one hand, there are many musicians who fervently believe that Stravinsky's third period is the ultimate, inevitable fulfillment of a lifelong artistic evolution. These musicians feel strongly that Stravinsky has produced music of transcendent quality; music finally denuded of overstuffed costumes and meretricious jewelry, purged of hysterics and emotional exhibitionism; music whose highest aesthetic value lies in its purity, objective beauty and restraint.

But just so strongly does the opposing camp believe that in this third period the genius of Stravinsky has entered upon senescence. These critics feel that the great weakness of Stravinsky's latest works rests in the consummate success with which the composer has achieved the ideal he has set for himself: to reduce the body of music to a mere ugly skeleton. Even in the most pretentious of his later works, they feel, there are stretches of tonal aridity, as well as a style that is effete and without character, devoid of any vital message.

However, though Stravinsky's music may be subject for violent difference of opinion, there can be no question that, for more than three decades, he has held a magisterial position over the composers of our time, exerting a cataclysmic influence upon the development of music. Just as in 1913, his cacophonies and his fresh rhythmic conceptions led the way to revolt and opened an altogether new avenue for musical expression (an avenue through which composers everywhere have followed his lead), so five years later his purity of writing pointed the way to a neo-classicism which many younger and older composers were to adopt just as readily. His outlook, his artistic aim, his style may undergo complete reversal, but such is the force and strength of his personality that he sways with him half of the music-world. Whether one accepts the music of his later period or rejects it, one cannot deny that as an influence in modern music Stravinsky remains unique.

Igor Stravinsky is small and thin; his chest appears hollow. His face, long and lean, has an expression of indefinable sadness. His eyes have a particularly piercing intensity that not even heavy lenses can obscure. An aquiline nose descends sharply from a majestic brow, and overlooks lips of uncompromising firmness. Upon his upper lip the hair grows thin and sparse as though he had only just begun to raise a moustache. He gives the impression of excessive fragileness. However, he is not half so susceptible to illness as his puny body suggests or as he himself frankly believes. An inveterate hypochondriac, his frequent pains and indispositions are often more imaginary than actual.

When this author last visited Stravinsky, the composer was living in a spacious apartment in the Faubourg St. Honoré district of Paris, a few moments from the Champs Elysées. The family consists of four children: the two boys are Feodor, a capable painter, and Sviatoslav, a competent pianist (who, together with his father, gave the world première of the *Concerto for two pianos* in Paris in October of 1935); the two girls are Milena, who paints icons for churches, and Milka, who is still very young.

Stravinsky impresses friends and those with whom he comes into direct contact as a man of Herculean energy. He is no longer a young man, and he has had a vigorous life. Yet his schedule would tax the endurance of one many years younger. His conductorial assignments force him to span virtually half a globe during a season. Yet he returns from each rigorous concert schedule and fatiguing succession of boats and trains as fresh as when he started—fresh enough, certainly, to hurl himself with his customary zest into producing a new composition, studying of new scores, increasing his musical equipment, perhaps even writing critical essays, or a book of memoirs.

Seated at his side, one instantly feels the enormous vitality of the man. He pours as much energy and zest into a casual conversation as he does into any of his endeavors—vigorously criticizing composers and their music, acridly condemning fads and fashions, electrically alive at every moment. As he talks, he diverts some of this endless energy into smoking cigarettes, stroking his moustache, and making staccato gestures of the wrists to punctuate his remarks. Occasionally, he shifts nervously in his chair, or paces the room. He seems incapable of being still a moment. He literally exhausts his listeners.

Stravinsky is enormously fond of conversation, and will discuss any musical subject with animation. Unless he is very familiar with his visitor, Stravinsky maintains a discreet but frigid silence where his own music is concerned. Not that Stravinsky is modest! As a matter of fact, he is quite convinced of the ultimate importance of his work, and has no hesitation in telling you about it; at one time he went so far as to say (refusing, however, to be specific) that there have been only three people in the world who have really understood his music—thereby placing his life work in the esoteric class of Whitehead's symbolic logic and Einstein's theory of relativity. His reluctance to discuss his own work springs from lifelong experience, which has taught him that the majority of those who come to him with idolatrous words on their lips reveal, when they flower into more elaborate conversation, an appalling ignorance of what he has tried to accomplish. If, however, Stravinsky feels that you possess an intelligent understanding of his scores, not only will he talk at length about his aims and ideals, but he will also have no hesitancy in telling you that his style has undergone a subtle and inevitable evolution, that his present neo-classical period is his most important phase and that the music world is not as yet sufficiently equipped to recognize the inherent greatness of his best works, among which he numbers *Oedipus Rex*, the *Symphonie des Psaumes* and *Perséphone*.

A musical conversation with Stravinsky is an invigorating experience if for no other reason than the unorthodoxy of his opinions. He esteems Donizetti and Bellini higher than he does Beethoven, Schubert, or Brahms. About Bellini he once said that the music world is still too immature to appreciate the real genius that created *Norma* and *La Sonnambula*. Wagner he detests instinctively and intellectually. His favorite composers include Mozart and Tchaikovsky. Among the moderns, he holds the highest esteem for Prokofiev, Hindemith and de Falla. None of the younger talents has made an impression upon him.

Stravinsky's world, however, does not consist entirely and completely of music. His intellectual horizon is sufficiently broad to include a keen appreciation of art and literature. Except for art, religion plays the most important role in his life. He is devoutly pious. In a corner of his study there hangs a painted icon over a lighted candle; in front of this Stravinsky prays each morning. He also attends the Russian Church in Paris regularly. By nature he is a mystic, believing firmly in his intuition and instincts and the power of heaven-sent inspiration. He is also morbidly superstitious.

There is nothing of the ascetic in Stravinsky. He is extraordinarily fond of good food and fine wines. Everything about him attests to his love for system and order. He dresses with the utmost neatness, his dress including spats, discreet jewelry, and a walking-stick. His daily life in Paris is systematically routinized to include not only his musical activities and his many appointments, but also his religious functions and even his regular gymnastic exercises before an open window. His desk is as neatly in shape after he has worked there for several hours as when he approaches it. A manuscript of his is the last word in precise and fastidious clarity; his calligraphy resembles fine print.

He detests theories concocted to explain his music. "A nose is not manufactured; a nose just is. Thus, too, my art," he once remarked to an interviewer. "For me, as a creative musician, composition is a daily function that I feel impelled to discharge," he wrote in his autobiography. "I compose because I am made for that and cannot do otherwise."

Printed in Great Britain
by Amazon